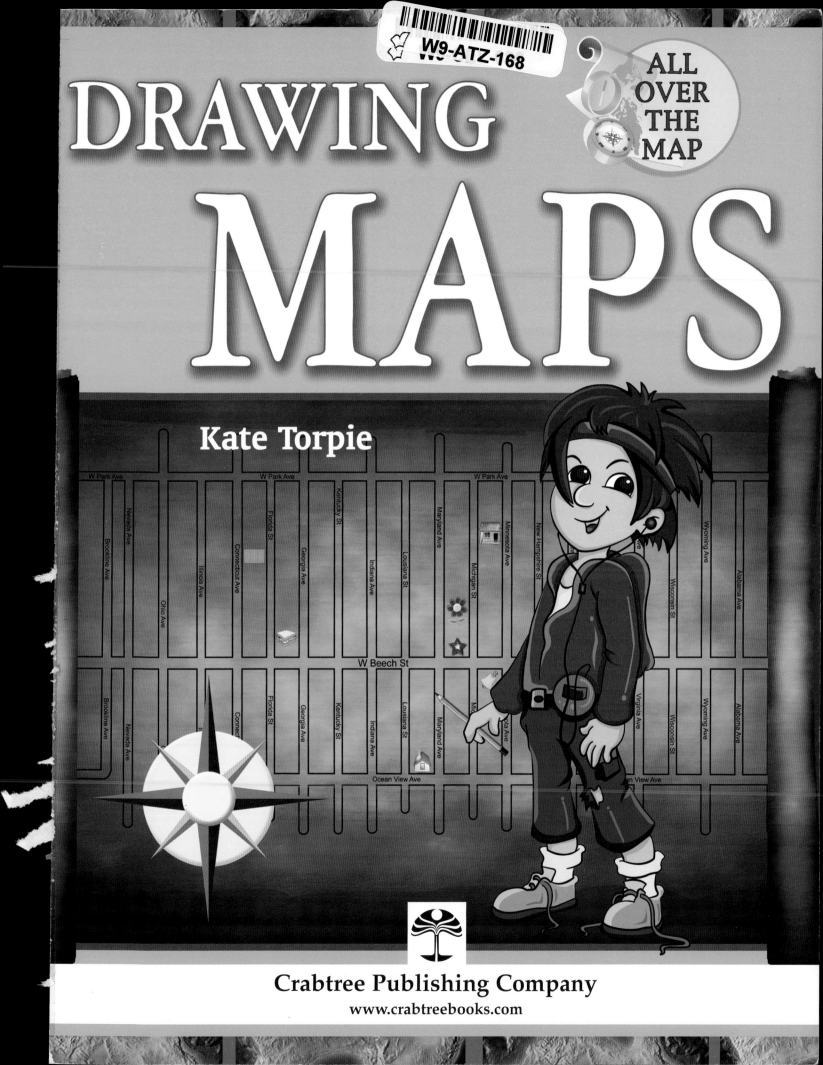

DRAWING MAPS

ALL OVER THE MAP

Kate Torpie

Crabtree Publishing Company

www.crabtreebooks.com

Crabtree Publishing Company

www.crabtreebooks.com

Author: Kate Torpie
Coordinating editor: Chester Fisher
Series editor: Scholastic Ventures
Project editor: Robert Walker
Editor: Reagan Miller
Proofreaders: Molly Aloian, Crystal Sikkens
Production coordinator: Katherine Kantor
Prepress technicians: Katherine Kantor, Ken Wright
Project manager: Santosh Vasudevan (Q2AMEDIA)
Art direction: Rahul Dhiman (Q2AMEDIA
Cover design: Ranjan Singh (Q2AMEDIA)
Design: Dibakar Acharjee (Q2AMEDIA)
Photo research: Ekta Sharma (Q2AMEDIA)

Photographs:
Fotolia: Marc Cecchetti: cover (center)
Istockphoto: Egor Mopanko: cover (top left, bottom left)
Map Resources: p. 19, 30–31
Mapsofworld.com: p. 26–27
Nationalatlas.gov: p. 16, 20–21, 31 (top right)
Shutterstock: Argus: p. 1, 5 (map), 7, 9, 10–11; Cora Reed: p. 4–5;
    Dragon_fang: cover (right); Gabriel Moisa: cover (background);
    Piks: cover (bottom)
United States Federal Government: p. 28–29

Illustrations:
Q2AMedia

Library and Archives Canada Cataloguing in Publication

Torpie, Kate, 1974-
    Drawing maps / Kate Torpie.

(All over the map)
Includes index.
ISBN 978-0-7787-4267-8 (bound).--ISBN 978-0-7787-4272-2 (pbk.)

1. Map drawing--Juvenile literature. I. Title.
II. Series: All over the map (St. Catharines, Ont.)

GA130.T67 2008   j526   C2008-904950-0

Library of Congress Cataloging-in-Publication Data

Torpie, Kate, 1974-
    Drawing maps / Kate Torpie.
       p. cm. -- (All over the map)
    Includes index.
    ISBN-13: 978-0-7787-4272-2 (pbk. : alk. paper)
    ISBN-10: 0-7787-4272-5 (pbk. : alk. paper)
    ISBN-13: 978-0-7787-4267-8 (reinforced library binding : alk. paper)
    ISBN-10: 0-7787-4267-9 (reinforced library binding : alk. paper)
    1. Map drawing--Juvenile literature. I. Title. II. Series.

    GA130.T67 2008
    526--dc22
                                                           2008033585

Crabtree Publishing Company

www.crabtreebooks.com   1-800-387-7650

Published in Canada
Crabtree Publishing
616 Welland Ave.
St. Catharines, Ontario
L2M 5V6

Published in the United States
Crabtree Publishing
PMB16A
350 Fifth Ave., Suite 3308
New York, NY 10118

Published in the United Kingdom
Crabtree Publishing
White Cross Mills
High Town, Lancaster
LA1 4XS

Published in Australia
Crabtree Publishing
386 Mt. Alexander Rd.
Ascot Vale (Melbourne)
VIC 3032

CONTENTS

Ahoy, Matey!

Hi! My name is Max. I want to be a cartographer. A cartographer is a person who creates maps. They get to draw and learn about different places at the same time. You have to know a little about maps to draw them. I just happen to know a little about maps that I can show you!

I buried some treasure for you to find! But first you need a treasure map. Let's make one.

This is the treasure map I have so far. Do you think it looks like a pirate's map? The map is not very good yet. It needs a **title**. The title tells the reader what the map is about.

It's hard to tell that this is a map. I think it needs a title. I'll call it "SECRET TREASURE MAP!"

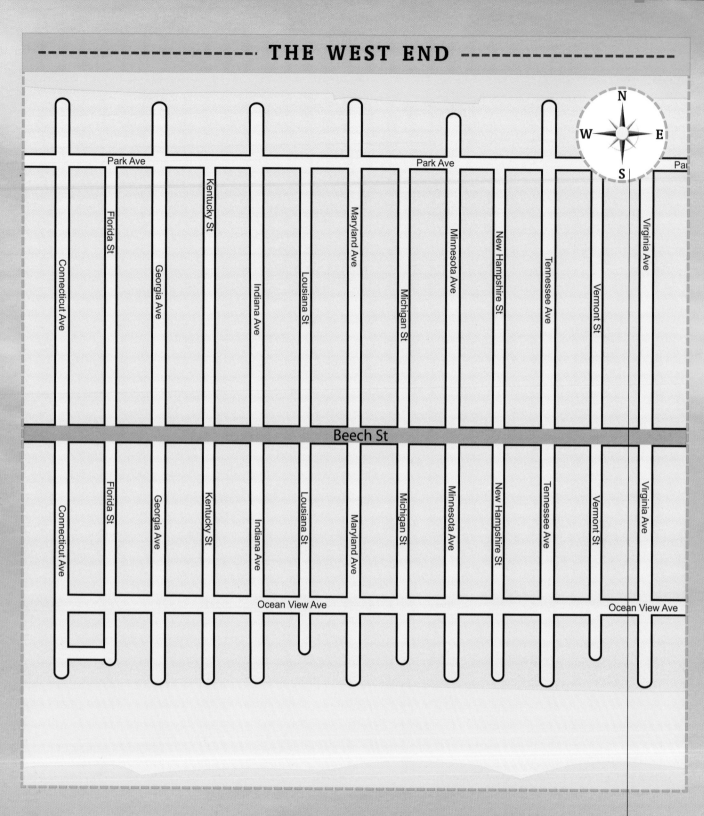

This is a map. It has details that make it useful, such as street names. Our map needs details. Otherwise you'll never find the treasure!

This **compass rose** shows you north, south, east, and west. My neighborhood is called the West End because it is to the west of town. Which way is west?

Now our map looks much better! This is because I added all the labels that were on the map of the West End.

SECRET TREASURE MAP

W Park Ave
W Park Ave
W Park Ave

W Beech St

Ocean View Ave
Ocean View Ave

N
W ● E
S

This map is broken into boxes called a grid. Each row has a letter. Each column has a number. My Uncle Jack lives in box C3. Look for row C. Now find column 3. The box where they meet is C3. That's where my uncle lives!

What box shows my house? First, name the letter of the row it is in. Then, tell what column it is in.

Our map is coming together. It has a title, a compass rose, and details to help you find your way.

Symbols and Legends

One of the things we learned in school is that maps can either be **simple** or **complex**. Complex maps have a lot more detail than simple maps do.

We added detail to our treasure map. But when a map has a lot of details, **symbols** and a **legend** make it easier to read. A symbol is a shape that is code for a building or place. The legend is the decoder for the symbols.

Let's look at some symbols that we might use.

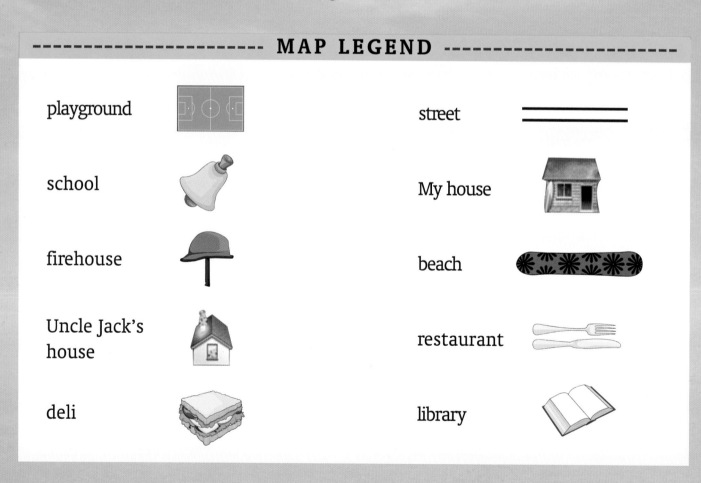

-------------------- MAP LEGEND --------------------

playground		street	
school		My house	
firehouse		beach	
Uncle Jack's house		restaurant	
deli		library	

Our map on page 7 was simple. This one is more complex. That means it shows more information. We used symbols to fit some details onto the map. Can you imagine if I tried to draw and label EACH house? The map would be really crowded!

SECRET TREASURE MAP

Columns: 1 2 3 4 5 6
Rows: A B C D

Street labels visible on map: Park Ave, Beech St, Ocean View Ave, Nevada Ave, Brookline Ave, Ohio Ave, Illinois Ave, Connecticut Ave, Florida St, Georgia Ave, Kentucky St, Indiana Ave, Louisiana St, Maryland Ave, Michigan St, Minnesota Ave, New Hampshire St, Tennessee Ave, Vermont St, Virginia Ave, Wisconsin St, Wyoming Ave, Alabama Ave

Compass: N, E, S, W

---------- **MAP LEGEND** ----------

playground		deli	
school		library	
My house		street	═══
Uncle Jack's house		restaurant	

Look at the legend. All the symbols on the map are explained here. Can you find my playground?

Our map is just about done. We should check it out to see if it is right.

Can you use our map to find the treasure? Follow the directions.
Remember to use the compass rose to help you find your way.

Don't forget to use
the compass rose!

1. Start at my house on Wyoming Ave.

2. Go north to Park Ave.

3. Turn west on Park Ave. Go past the deli.

4. Turn south on Maryland Ave.

5. Continue on Maryland Ave. to the library on Beech St.

6. Turn west on Beech St.

7. Follow Beech St. to Florida St.

8. Turn north on Florida St.

9. The treasure is buried in the playground. Start digging!

Name the grid location where the treasure is buried.

Going Places

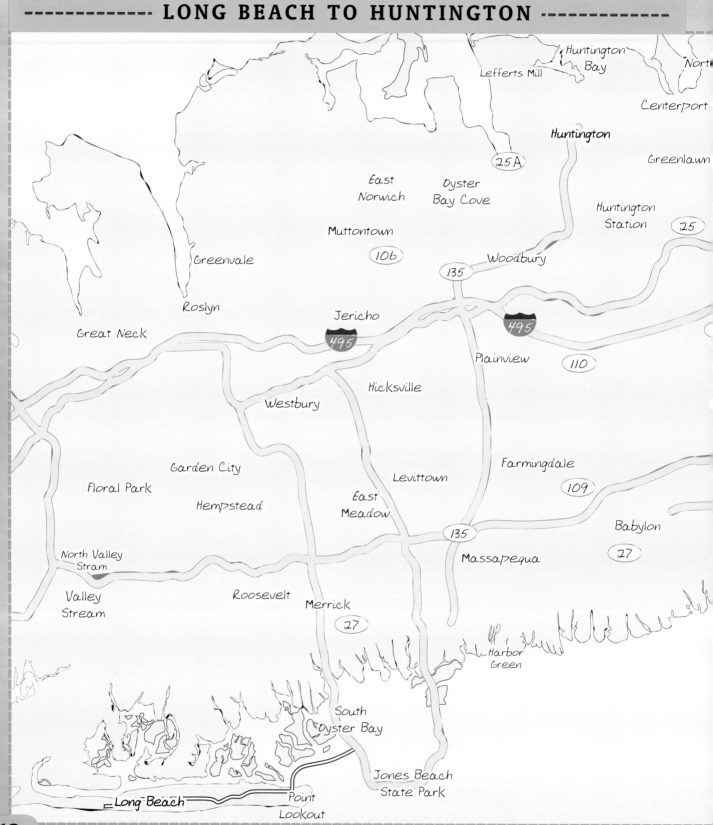

Lefferts Mill

Huntington Bay

Nort

Centerport

Huntington

Greenlawn

25A

East Norwich

Oyster Bay Cove

Huntington Station

25

Muttontown

106

Woodbury

135

Greenvale

Roslyn

Jericho

495

495

Plainview

110

Great Neck

Hicksville

Westbury

Farmingdale

109

Garden City

Levittown

Floral Park

East Meadow

Babylon

Hempstead

135

27

North Valley Stram

Massapequa

Valley Stream

Roosevelt

Merrick

27

Harbor Green

South Oyster Bay

Jones Beach State Park

Long Beach

Point Lookout

12

Now we know how to draw maps that show paths. That means we can make road maps! A road map is a map that shows the roads and streets in an area. I want to make a map from Long Beach to Huntington. Here's the directions I can remember and a map.

Directions to Vincent's House

1. Take Park Avenue to a highway.

2. Take that highway to another one.

3. Take the other one north.

4. Get off that highway and go east until Main St.

5. Look for Vincent's house.

Commack

495

r Park

Babylon

These directions would be hard to follow. A map would be better!

Map Facts

You already learned about some symbols. Symbols are used on road maps, too.

More Maps

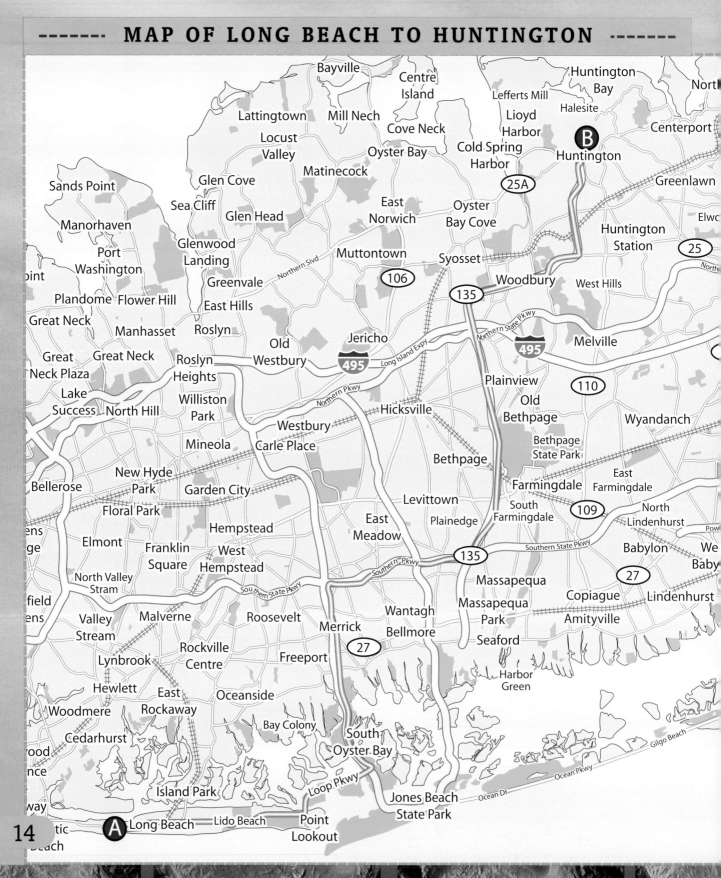

My directions were not very helpful. I didn't give clear information. Look at THIS map. It shows the same area as the map on pages 12-13. It has details and symbols that we could use.

-- MAP LEGEND --

▭	Interstate Highways
▭	Other Highways
┼┼┼┼┼┼	Railroad
▭	Water
▭	Parks

Road maps should show the names of highways and other roads.

A map can be clearer than just giving someone directions.

This is a **scale**. It shows you how to read distance on a map. For example, on this map, every inch stands for 5 km in real life.

This map tells you to start at point A and end at point B. That's important if you needed directions. Point A is where you start. Point B is where you finish.

15

Do you think you could a draw map of a bigger area? We learned about drawing state maps in school. I'll show you how!

I live in New York State. You can draw your state.

1. Give your map a title. I'll call mine "New York State." Your title should be the name of your state.

2. Find a map of your state. Here is a map of my state.

NEW YORK STATE

What does your state look like?

16

3. Trace the shape of your state onto a piece of paper. Here's what mine looks like.

4. Outline your state with one color. Try to make your outline as neat as possible. The outline shows the state **boundary**. A boundary separates one place from another.

5. Color in your state. Choose a different color from the outline.

6. Draw a compass rose and legend. Look at the legend I drew for my map. It shows symbols for state boundaries and water. On maps, water is always the same blue color.

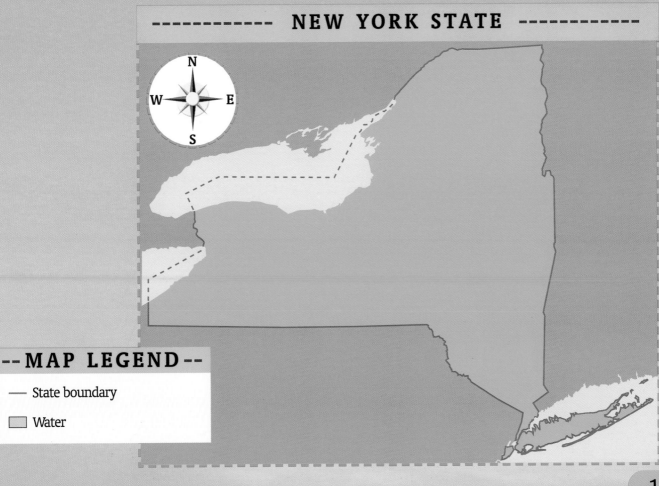

NEW YORK STATE

--MAP LEGEND--

— State boundary

☐ Water

Here is my map. How is your map coming along? I added details—you can, too. I included the Hudson River. I also included New York City, and my hometown of Long Beach.

NEW YORK STATE

Without this legend, you wouldn't understand any of the symbols on the map!

---- **MAP LEGEND** ----

〼	Hudson River
★	New York City
⌂	Long Beach
—	State boundary
▭	Water

Here is a complex map of New Your State. When you make
your map, you can make it as complex as you like.

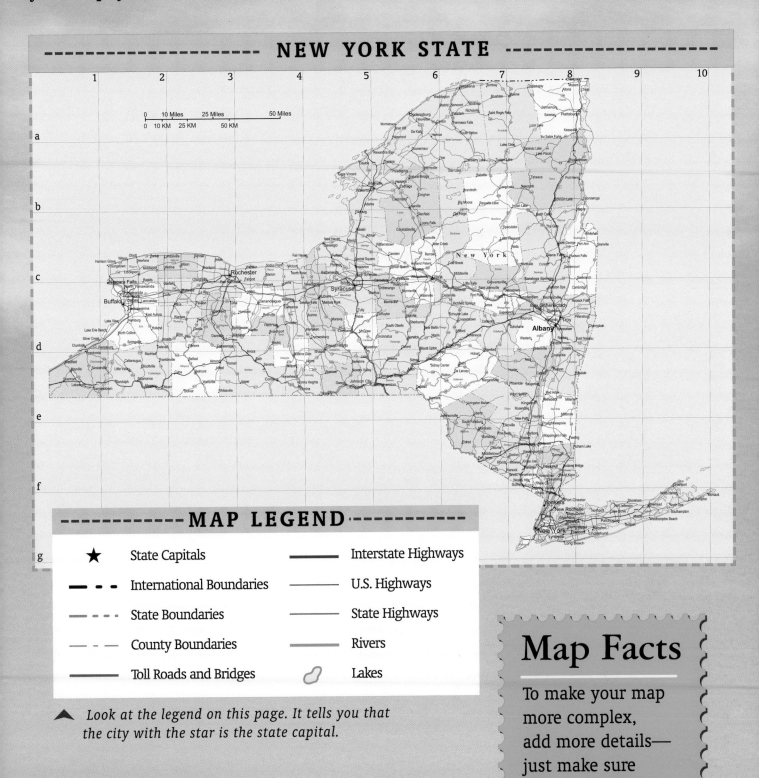

MAP LEGEND

★	State Capitals	——	Interstate Highways
– – –	International Boundaries	——	U.S. Highways
–·–·–	State Boundaries	——	State Highways
–·–·–	County Boundaries	——	Rivers
——	Toll Roads and Bridges	⬭	Lakes

▲ *Look at the legend on this page. It tells you that
the city with the star is the state capital.*

Use the legend to find my hometown. Tell me
what box on the letter-number grid it falls in!
Find the answer at the bottom of the page.

Map Facts

To make your map
more complex,
add more details—
just make sure
each is explained
in the legend.

USA All the WAY!

Drawing this map will be hard because it shows such a large area. Just remember to follow the same steps as you did drawing the road map and state map. Once you know how to draw a map, you can draw a map of ANY place!

-------------------------- **THE UNITED STATES** --------------------------

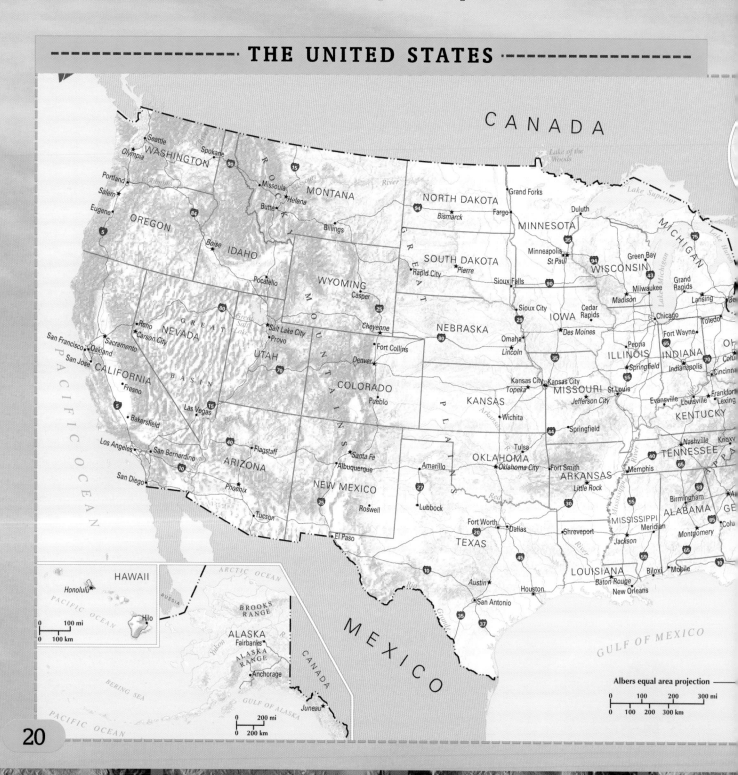

Map Facts

These states are far away from the other 48 states. Some maps show them in little boxes, so they are easier to see.

1. First, we should pick a title! Let's call the map "The United States."

2. Next, find a map that we can copy or trace. Take a good look at it. What do you see? It shows the United States, but it also shows a little of the countries around it. I see lakes and oceans, too.

A map is a smaller drawing of a big place. Remember that the scale shows you how big the land really is.

3. Now we trace the map onto another piece of paper.

4. Next, outline the countries so you can tell them apart. There's Mexico, Canada, and the United States. Boundaries between countries are international boundaries.

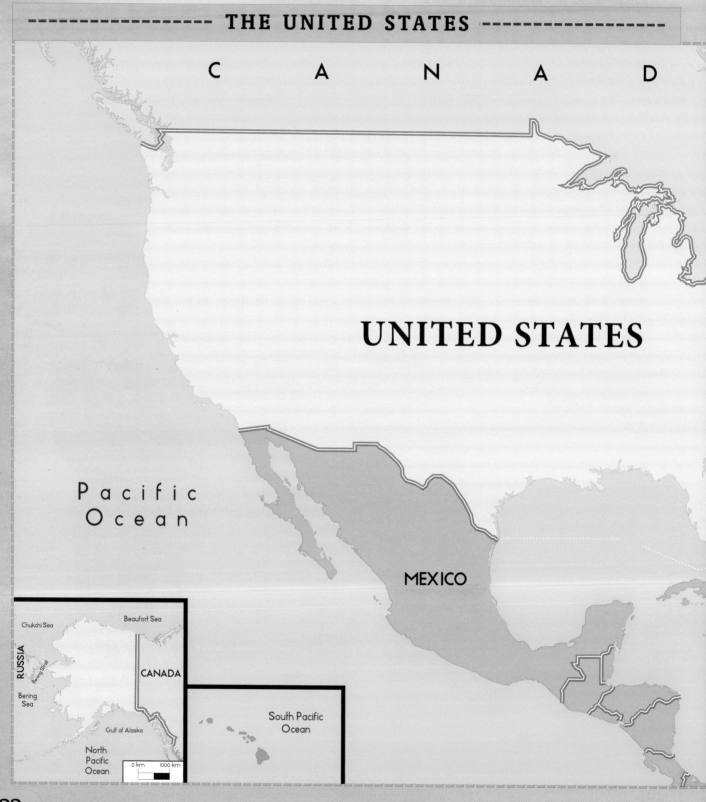

THE UNITED STATES

C A N A D

UNITED STATES

Pacific Ocean

MEXICO

Chukchi Sea

Beaufort Sea

RUSSIA

Bering Strait

CANADA

Bering Sea

Gulf of Alaska

North Pacific Ocean

South Pacific Ocean

0 km   1000 km

It's important that our map shows that there are three different countries here.

5. Let's label countries and oceans for now.

A

What symbol will I put in the legend for international boundaries?

Atlantic Ocean

My map looks pretty good!

6. Outline and color in the states. First, outline each state. It's easiest to trace their shapes. Color is how we tell the states apart. All touching states must be different colors.

7. Make the international boundaries a different color than any states or state boundaries.

8. Draw a compass rose and legend. Our legend shows symbols for state boundaries, international boundaries, and water.

N
W · E
S

C · A

Pacific
Ocean

Chukchi Sea

Beaufort Sea

RUSSIA

Bering Strait

CANADA

Bering
Sea

Gulf of Alaska

North
Pacific
Ocean

0 km   1000 km

South Pacific
Ocean

Good job! Do you want to add more details? Let's look at a map with a lot of details. Maybe you'll get some ideas!

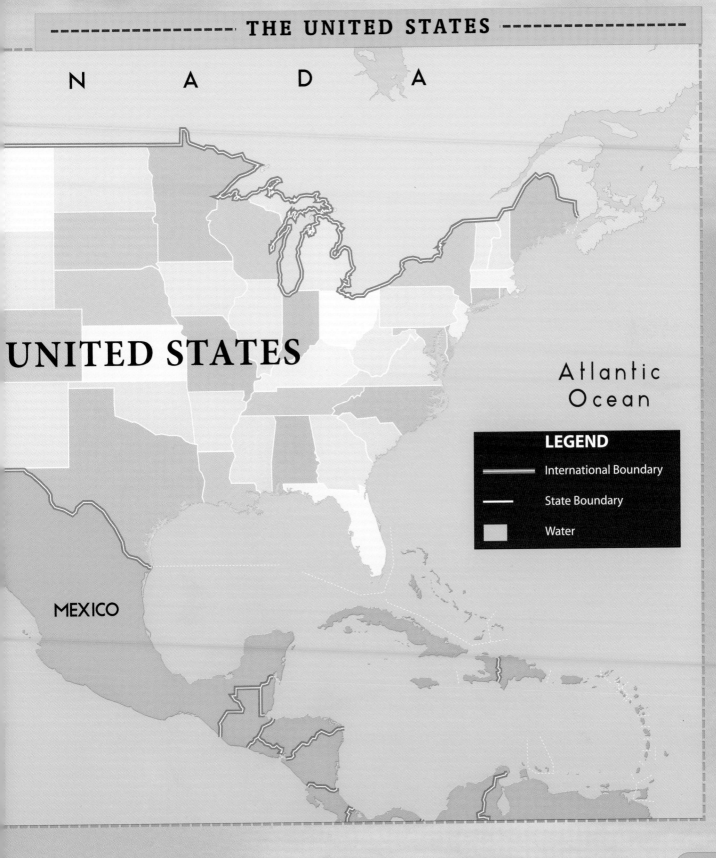

THE UNITED STATES

N A D A

UNITED STATES

Atlantic Ocean

MEXICO

LEGEND

International Boundary

State Boundary

Water

This map has a lot more detail! It is a road map of the entire U.S. You can include all of it, or just the parts you choose.

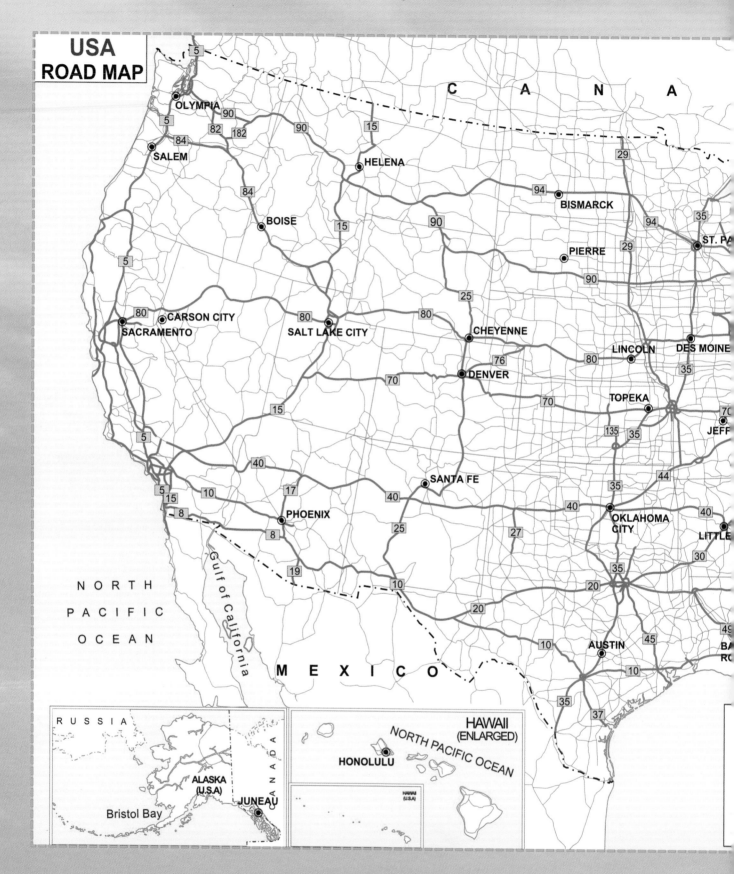

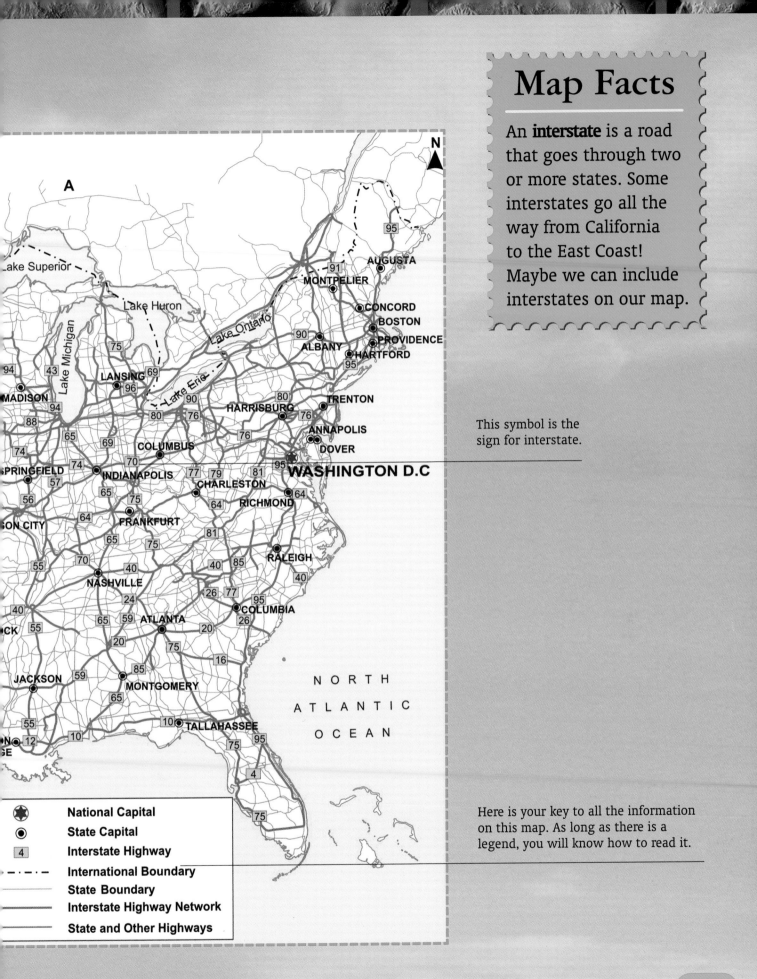

Map Facts

An **interstate** is a road that goes through two or more states. Some interstates go all the way from California to the East Coast! Maybe we can include interstates on our map.

This symbol is the sign for interstate.

Here is your key to all the information on this map. As long as there is a legend, you will know how to read it.

A

Lake Superior

Lake Huron

Lake Michigan

Lake Ontario

Lake Erie

AUGUSTA

MONTPELIER

CONCORD

BOSTON

ALBANY

PROVIDENCE

HARTFORD

TRENTON

HARRISBURG

ANNAPOLIS

DOVER

COLUMBUS

WASHINGTON D.C

MADISON

LANSING

SPRINGFIELD

INDIANAPOLIS

CHARLESTON

RICHMOND

ON CITY

FRANKFURT

RALEIGH

NASHVILLE

COLUMBIA

ATLANTA

CK

JACKSON

MONTGOMERY

TALLAHASSEE

NORTH ATLANTIC OCEAN

Legend

- ★ National Capital
- ◉ State Capital
- 4 Interstate Highway
- —·—·— International Boundary
- —— State Boundary
- —— Interstate Highway Network
- —— State and Other Highways

27

The World
According to You!

When you know how to draw a map, the whole world can be yours! You can draw a map that is as complex as you want.

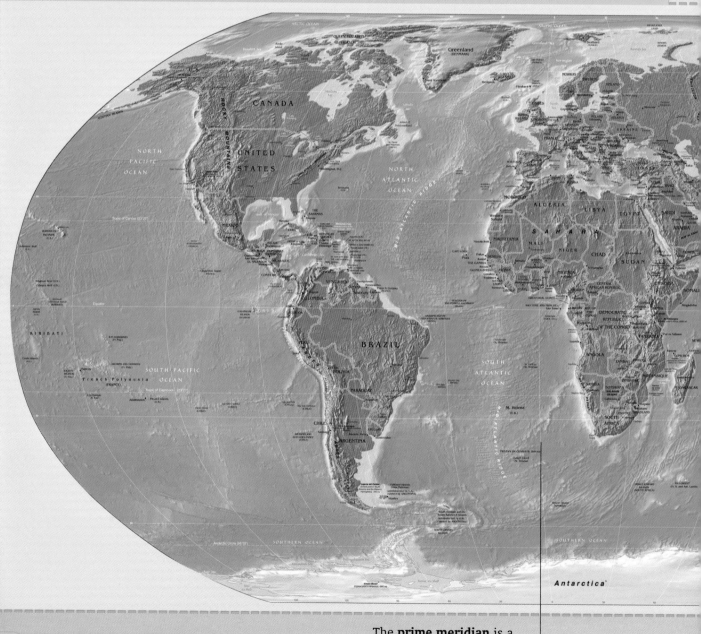

The **prime meridian** is a line that wraps from north to south around the planet.

This is a **physical** map of the world. It doesn't show countries. It just shows information about the land and water on Earth. Colors on this map are code for how the land is shaped.

The **equator** is an imaginary line that wraps from west to east around the planet.

How to Make Any Map

1. Pick a title.

2. Find a picture of the area you want to draw.

3. Copy or trace it. That includes outlining countries, states, or even continents!

4. Draw a compass rose and legend.

5. Add details. Make sure to add symbols to the legend.

This map does not have a compass rose. Which way is north?

Maps can show the same place but include different information. Here is another map of the world. This is a **political** map. A political map shows countries, not physical features. The continents are divided into countries.

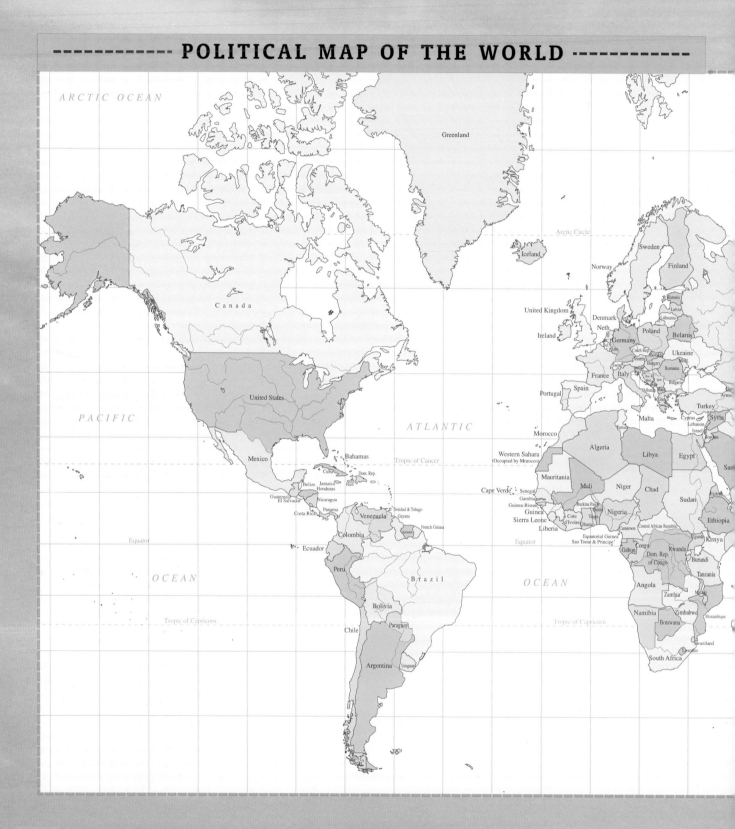

POLITICAL MAP OF THE WORLD

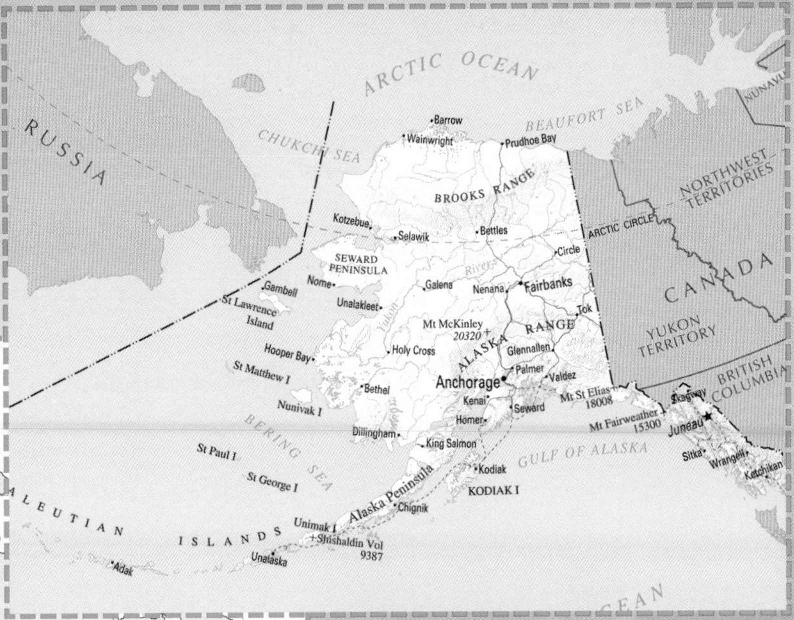

Map Labels — Alaska inset

ARCTIC OCEAN

RUSSIA

CHUKCHI SEA

BEAUFORT SEA

NUNAVUT

• Barrow
• Wainwright
• Prudhoe Bay

BROOKS RANGE

NORTHWEST TERRITORIES

Kotzebue •
• Selawik
• Bettles
ARCTIC CIRCLE

SEWARD PENINSULA
• Circle

• Gambell
Nome •
• Galena Nenana
★ Fairbanks

St Lawrence Island
River

CANADA

• Unalakleet
• Tok

Hooper Bay •
Mt McKinley 20320 ft
RANGE

ALASKA

YUKON TERRITORY

St Matthew I •
• Holy Cross

Nunivak I •
• Bethel
★ Anchorage
• Glennallen
• Palmer

Kenai •
★ • Valdez
Mt St Elias 18008

BRITISH COLUMBIA

• Homer
Seward •

• Dillingham
• King Salmon

St Paul I •
Skagway •
Mt Fairweather 15300
Juneau ★

St George I •
GULF OF ALASKA
Sitka •
Wrangell •

BERING SEA
KODIAK I
• Kodiak

• Chignik
Ketchikan •

ALEUTIAN ISLANDS
Unimak I
Alaska Peninsula

• Adak
Unalaska •
Shishaldin Vol 9387
OCEAN

Main map labels

ARCTIC OCEAN

Russia

Kazakhstan

Mongolia

Uzbekistan
Kyrgyzstan
Turkmenistan Tajikistan

N. Korea

Iran

China

S. Korea Japan

Afghanistan

PACIFIC

Qatar
U.A.E.
Pakistan

Nepal Bhutan
Bangladesh

Tropic of Cancer

Oman

India

Burma Laos

OCEAN

Somalia

Thailand Cambodia Vietnam

Philippines

Sri Lanka

Brunei

Palau

INDIAN

Malaysia

Equator

Indonesia

Papua New Guinea

Solomon Islands

East Timor

Mauritius

Vanuatu

Somoa

Fiji

Madagascar

Tropic of Capricorn

Australia

Tonga

OCEAN

New Zealand

0   1000 Km

▶ Maps are flat pictures of a round Earth. This makes it hard to draw the world perfectly. On one map, Russia looks far away from the United States. Russia and Alaska are really less than three miles apart!

Activity

Use the map to find a country that is about the same size as the United States.

31

Glossary

Note: Some boldfaced words are defined where they appear in the book.

boundary A border between states and countries

compass rose A map part that shows north, south, east, and west

complex Having a lot of details or information

equator The line that circles Earth from east to west

interstate A highway that goes between two or more states

legend A key to decode symbols on a map

physical Having to do with the land

political Having to do with countries

prime meridian A special line that circles Earth from north to south

scale A map part that shows you how to read distance on a map

simple Not having a lot of details or information

symbol A shape that represents a building, place, or other part on a map

title The name of a map that tells you what it will show

Index

Printed in the U.S.A. - CG